W9-BSR-080

doll
Hair

Styling Tips and Tricks
for Your Dolls

American Girl®

Contents

Hair Care & Styling Stuff

Terrific Tails

Braid Parade

Twists and Turns

Dear Doll Lover,

Treat your doll to *salon-styled hair* without leaving your bedroom! Discover the do's and don'ts of keeping your doll's hair in *top-notch shape*. Learn the secrets of *perfect pigtails*, *elegant updos*, and dozens of other popular styles. Finally, find out how miniature *doodads* and other special accessories can keep your doll *sitting pretty*.

Heads Up!

Ready to start styling? Be sure to play it safe.

Style Starters

No matter what style you choose, be sure to read these important tips.

1 Keep your doll still. **Sit her between your legs or ask someone to hold her. Be sure you don't pull your doll's hair too hard when brushing, or her neck could come loose. If you can, hold her neck as you work.**

2 Never get your doll wet. **Water can damage a doll and rust her eyes, so protect her body and clothes with a plastic cape or towel, and hold your hand over her eyes when misting.**

3 For best results when styling, **lightly mist your doll's hair, then take a short section at the tip and work your way toward the scalp, using a doll hair wire brush. Plastic bristles snag hair.**

Wash and Wear

To avoid frizzies and other damage, don't wash your doll's hair. But if her hair gets dirty from play or by accident, follow these steps:

1 Cover your doll's eyes with a towel. Tip her head back under the faucet, and wet her hair with cool water. Be sure she's face-up so that water flows away from her eyes!

2 Using a mild shampoo, gently lather the doll's hair, then rinse until the water runs clear.

3 Lay the doll's head on a dry towel, then wrap the towel around her head, squeezing out excess water. Do not twist or rub!

4 Remove tangles from the ends to the roots so that you don't pull out hair. Let dry overnight, or, for quicker drying, place your doll in front of a cool fan.

Hot Topic

A doll's hair is made of a special plastic, and heat will frizz it—or even melt it! *Never* use a blow-dryer, curling iron, hot rollers, or other heat appliance on her hair.

Flip Tail

Flip for a new twist on the classic ponytail!

1 Make a low ponytail. Tie off with elastic.

2 Reach underneath the ponytail and use your finger and thumb to make a hole in the middle of the hair above the elastic.

3 With the other hand, twist the ponytail, grab it with the fingers that are making the hole, and pull it through.

Ponytail Wrap

Use a strand of hair to band a ponytail.

1 Make a low ponytail, leaving a small strand of hair underneath the tail out of the elastic.

2 Wrap the loose strand around the elastic 1 or 2 times, depending on doll's hair length.

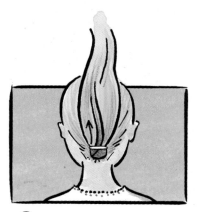

3 Tip the doll upside down, tuck the rest of the loose strand into the elastic under the ponytail, and pull through.

Pigtails and Ponies

High or low, top or side—give your doll a new look every day.

❋ Perky Pigtails

Gather your doll's hair on each side of her head at her ears and tie it off with matching elastics.

❋ Side Winder

Gather your doll's hair on one side and tie it off with an elastic.

❀ Partial Pony

Pull the top and sides of the hair to the crown and tie them up with a small scrunchie.

❀ High Style

Pull all the hair to the crown and wrap with an elastic. Add a scrunchie to accent an outfit.

Ponytail Veil

Weave your doll's hair into a pretty ponytail veil.

1 Make 3 mini ponytails on the crown: 1 in the middle, 1 on the right, and 1 on the left. Tie off with elastics.

2 Separate the middle ponytail into 2 sections.

3 Combine the right-hand section with the ponytail on the right and tie off with an elastic.

4 Combine the left-hand section with the ponytail on the left and tie off with an elastic.

5 Bring the 2 new ponytails to the center and make 1 big ponytail. Tie off with an elastic.

Super Style

Try starting this style with 5 mini ponies, as seen in the photo at left. You'll have another layer when you're finished!

Stylist Secret

Rubber bands for braces work best!

11

Pony Detail

Dress up pint-size ponytails with bitty baubles.

Lace It Up

Wrap a ponytail with satin or leather cord. First, make a ponytail. Tie it off with elastics at the top and bottom. Wrap the center of the cord around the top elastic 3 times, then crisscross the ends every inch or so as you move down. Tie a small bow around the bottom elastic. **Note:** Be sure that your doll's hair is dry, or the dye from the cord could bleed onto it.

Twinkle Tail

Add sparkle to a ponytail with mini clips, Velcro stick-ons, or spring coils. Just make a pony, fluff up the tail, and clip on a sprinkling of twinkling jewels.

Rainbow Row

Create a colorful rainbow down a pretty ponytail. Wrap with 2 different colors of elastics around a low pony. Move down a few inches, and repeat. Continue down the length of the entire tail.

Beautiful Braids

Brush up on your braiding basics.

1 Make a part down the back of your doll's head for pigtails.

2 Tie off 1 pigtail. Separate hair from the other pigtail into 3 equal sections.

3 Cross the section on your right over the center section.

4 Cross the section on your left over the center section.
Tip: Keep a tight hold on sections as you cross them.

5 Continue crossing over the center section with left and right sections until hair is braided. Tie off with an elastic and repeat on the other side.

Stylist Secret

Always mist your doll's hair with water from a spray bottle before braiding to keep her style flyaway-free.

French Braids

Practice makes perfect with this classic style!

1 Make a part down the back of the head for pigtails. Use an elastic to hold one section off to the side.

2 On the other side, gather hair from the front of the head and separate it into 3 even sections.

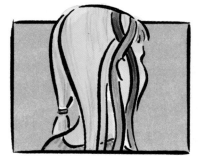

3 Begin by crossing over the sections once, like you would in a regular braid.

4 Grab a few strands of hair to the left of the braid and add to the left-hand section. Cross the section over the center.

5 Grab a few strands of hair to the right of the braid and add to the right-hand section. Cross the section over the center.

6 Repeat until all hair has been added, then continue with a regular braid. Tie off with an elastic. Repeat on the other side.

Braid Craze

Make one braid for fun or half a dozen for drama!

✿ Tiara Braid

Try a French braid across the head. Instead of pulling hair from left and right, pull it from front and back.

✿ Braid Shower

Separate hair into 5 even sections, and hold it in place with mini clips. French braid each section to the crown, then tie off with an elastic. Continue the braids down the back.

❀ Front Row

Separate hair into 5 even sections, and hold it in place with mini clips. French braid each section to the crown, then replace the clip.

❀ Drop Braids

Braid 3 small sections of hair on each side of the head. Tie off each braid with an elastic. Tip: Use special accessories on the front braids!

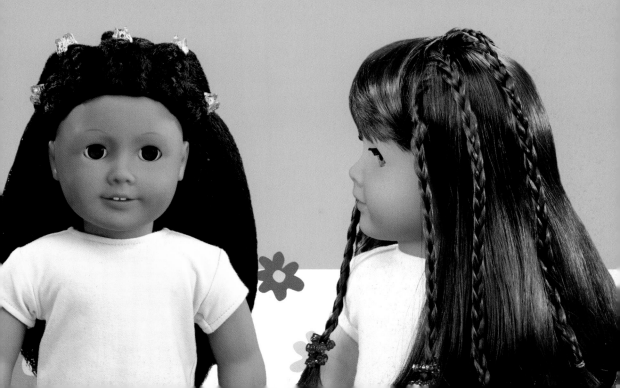

Rope Braid

Twist your doll's hair into a rope.

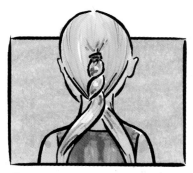

1 Brush hair back into a high ponytail. Tie off with an elastic.

2 Separate the ponytail into 2 equal sections.

3 Tightly cross one section over the other until you reach the end of the ponytail. Tie off with another elastic.

All-Star Braids

Try these neat braids to help your doll beat the heat.

1 Make low pigtails and tie off with elastics. Divide *each* pigtail into 3 even sections.

2 Braid each section and tie off with an elastic.

3 After braiding, remove the 3 elastics, then hold all 3 braids together and tie off with 1 elastic. Repeat on the other side.

Ballet Bun

Twirl your dancing doll's hair into an elegant bun.

1 Gather hair at the back of the doll's head and make a high ponytail. Tie off with an elastic.

2 Twist ponytail tightly, spritzing it with water to keep shorter ends from popping out.

3 Wrap twisted ponytail around the elastic.

4 Tuck the end of the ponytail under the coil, or bun, and insert a hairpin or bobby pin to hold.

5 Pin the rest of the bun in place, crisscrossing pins and grabbing hair from the scalp and the bun.

Stylist Secret

U-shaped hairpins work best for keeping thick doll hair in a bun. Press the pins deep into the hair and they won't show much. For thinner doll hair, use bobby pins.

Nifty Knots

Twist your doll's hair into "teddy bear" ears.

1 Make 2 high pigtails and tie off with elastics. **Starting on one side, twist pigtail until it begins to coil up on itself.**

2 Coil the pigtail around itself, and tuck the end underneath the coil.

3 Insert hairpins into the coil, crisscrossing them. Repeat on the other side.

Super Style

Make Nifty Knots at the nape of your doll's neck. Start with 2 low pigtails and twist, following Steps 2–3.

Twists and Turns

Go for fun or fancy with these hip flips!

❁ Pigtail Twist

Try this style on nearly any length of hair. Part hair down the middle. Twist the front sides up away from the face, then pull them into pigtails with the rest of the hair. Tie off with elastics.

❁ Twisty Bun

Make 2 high pigtails and tie off with elastics. Twist each pigtail into a coil. Hold in place with mini clips. If desired, use pins to tuck away stray hairs.

❀ Curly Top

This style works only on dolls with short, curly hair. Pull hair into a high ponytail. Tie with an elastic. Spread hair around elastic.

❀ Back Flip

Make a partial ponytail by pulling the sides and top of the hair to the back. Tie off with an elastic. Flip the ponytail over itself 1 or 2 times.

Do the Twist

Sweep your doll's hair off her shoulders for an elegant look.

1 Gather hair at the back of your doll's head, as if you were making a low ponytail.

2 Twist hair to the end while slowly pulling up, making a roll. Tip: Mist with water to tame stray hairs.

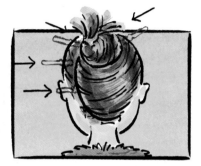

3 Insert hairpins around the coil and the roll to hold in place.

Super Style

Follow Steps 1 and 2. Hold hair up and clamp a jaw clip onto the middle of the roll.

Hair Thingies

Add sparkle to your doll's style with clips, barrettes, and more!

Doll-ing Doodads!

Beautiful barrettes, shiny scrunchies, and fantastic elastics can add sparkle to almost any doll hairdo. But choose accessories carefully. Some hair thingies can slip out of slick doll hair, and sharp metal clasps can break or damage hair. Also, be sure elastics are covered so they're snag-free.

Quick and Cool

Bandannas, headbands, and jaw clips are quick and pretty hair fixes. For this simple style, slide a bandanna underneath the doll's hair, pull the sides up, and tie them in a knot. Slide the knot to the side.

Get Creative

Spice up your doll's hair with out-of-the-ordinary accessories. Try out cool hair chopsticks. Attach a fancy bow to a plain headband. Decorate bobby pins with rhinestones, buttons, bows, or beads.